Little Worlds

Written by
Louis Alan Swartz

Illustrated by
Diane Woods

Hugo House

Hugo House Publishers, LTD.

Little Worlds: Constructed of Magic: VOLUME 3

ISBN: 978-1-948261-23-4
Library of Congress Control Number: 2014959925

Cover, interior design, illustrations and photos: Diane
Woods and other artists,
www.dianewoodsdesign.com

Interior Layout: Ronda Taylor,
www.heartworkpublishing.com

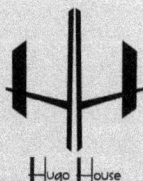

Hugo House

Hugo House Publishers, Ltd.
Denver, Colorado
Austin, Texas
www.HugoHousePublishers.com

Dedication

I dedicate this work to L. Ron Hubbard, author, philosopher and educator from whose writings I first gained certainty of myself and all of humankind as immortal spiritual beings.

In Praise of Little Worlds

Reading it was like floating in a cool pool on a hot day. I am most happy to be able to share the not-so-small worlds of my two dear friends.
—Wendy Negley

The aesthetics of this book is undeniable. The illustrator perfectly puts into the visual world that which the poet conjures in our minds. I find reading this work relaxing and it takes me on a journey to my own little worlds. Definitely a good book to have on the lamp table as one unwinds for the day.
—Tree Nebeker

Beautiful, wonderful, enchanting! Thank you.
—David I. Minkoff M.D.

Louis Swartz has a unique ability to bridge two very different worlds—the spiritual and the material. It is done with gentle yet powerful language, and illuminated with ethereal imagery. His writings speak softly to all that you are—and all that you will be.
—Barbara Anne Dunn

You've really created a masterpiece here.
—Sisu Raiken

I beyond love it. The aesthetic wavelength oozes from the pages, both the words and illustrations. A true masterpiece.
THIS MUST BE SHARED WITH THE WORLD!
—Bernard Percy

With this rough and tumble life it is so easy to get caught in the mechanics of a life. Reading Little Worlds recreates for me my knowledge that it is not the 'things' of a life that create it, but the pursuit of kindness, beauty and joy. Indeed, these writings remind me that I am immortal and that I am magic and can create anything I like! I kept coming back to select pages after a rough day and was completely inspired newly each time. This is the sort of book you leave out on your coffee table or bedside and re-immerse yourself in with regularity.
—Barbara Russell

The creation of beauty is the best there is in man—I believe you have really hit that mark!
—Lance Whalin

So the first thing I noticed was that I was transported. The words conjure images, remembrances, hopes for future—and the art—black and white is perfect.
—Terry Garcia

Staggeringly beautiful, real, genuine. Sets an ideal ... and transports you there.
—Barbara Miller

I have just finished reading Little Worlds, the latest book of poetry and prose, by Louis Swartz. I read it cover to cover, nonstop. It was like walking along an alpine lake, marveling at the reflections of the rest of the world.

Louis has this wonderful ability to say things that reflect my own life. There is a profound wisdom couched in the simplicity and truthfulness of the words.

I have never seen the spirituality of life, living and death so clearly and so lovingly expressed. I found myself thinking "By golly, that really is it!" repeatedly throughout the book. These are things you know or suspect as truths but have never been able to articulate with clarity.

And that, I think, is the power of Louis Swartz, the poet. He whispers these things in our ear and the calamity or the blindness in our own worlds become settled and serene. I am very happy that somehow within my eternity I have come upon this giant angel who consistently, steadfastly points toward the need for peace, love, kindness and our own immortality.
—Bill Johonnesson

WOW! I just looked through the book Little Worlds. I didn't have time yet to fully immerse myself in its glory at leisure, but I looked through all of it. It is profoundly spectacular. It takes my breath away.
—**Ingrid Gudenas**

This book transplants one into the ethereal world that we visualise in our mind's eye at times of revelation and exuberance. It lifts you to the beauty of existence and beyond the apparent reality of the world we inhabit as people in this sphere. Each page with its sensational artistry in words and images brings forth a happiness and calmness for life. A beautiful gift for oneself or a friend.
—**Cecile Vowles**

Just love it all. This little book Little Worlds is like carrying 'both worlds inside of me.' Thank you so much for such a beautiful heartfelt product! In the poem, "By the Way"—yes, I just may be immortal, by the way."... love these words! Wishing you the very best on your new book.
—**Mary Rensberry**

Contents

Chapter One
Spring

Chapter Two
Aesthetics

Chapter Three
Marriage, Family, Children

Chapter Four
Humanity

Chapter Five
America

Chapter Six
The Human Spirit

Chapter Seven
Old Age

Chapter Eight
Immortality

Preface

I am so pleased you are here opening *Little Worlds,* volume 3 of the *Constructed of Magic Trilogy.*

Little Worlds, these microcosms of human experience, belong to us and not to the physical universe. They are created in thought space and time with thought energy and things. They may describe the physical world but they do not belong to it. They are indestructible and immortal.

In *Constructed of Magic and Other Poems on the Immortality of the Human Spirit,* Louis Swartz shared a definition of *magic* as "having special powers that are not normal or natural so that you can do impossible things: something that creates wonderful or extraordinary effects".

Shortly before Louis wrote that in 2015, I had, quite unexpectedly, discovered just such a power after an earthquake had reduced the contents of my home to a shambles.

Following the earthquake, my grown daughter, Kenna, had stopped by for a visit. Ignoring the mess we sat for a while on the living room sofa facing the normal looking front wall.

After a bit we got the nerve to move to the dining room. Navigating around a fallen bookcase, we cleared a spot on the floor near the china cabinet which was on its back in the center of the room. It was surrounded by a sea of china bits and pieces. Aunt Mil had brought this back from Germany when I was a child, the china of holiday meals going back sixty years.

I picked up the only cup that remained whole, well almost, except for a tiny chip and a missing handle. Kenna said one word, "Chip!" Suddenly I could see and hear *Chip*, the adorable character in the movie, *Beauty and the Beast*.

With one word my magic child had transported me to a *Little World* of rhythm, harmony and grace where the tiny chipped cup asks *Beauty*, "Want to see me do a trick?" and the amazing company of candlesticks, dishes, steins and swimming spoons sing "Be our guest, be our guest ...!" in the magical tale we had enjoyed together again and again, We laughed together, and it was so good to laugh together.

Wanting to restore *Chip's* handle, I looked across the sea of debris containing his eleven broken brethren. A little framed photo of my Dad, Father Albert, Aunt Lou and Uncle Johnny was propped up against the table. A delicate handle lay just before them in the *china sea.* I retrieved it and held it up next to *Chip.* It fit!

  These are the kinds of *Little Worlds* that Louis celebrates in his poetry. In these amazing moments, we shine above the sea of broken bits below and create *Little Worlds* together out of our immortal love, humor, admiration, kindness, hope, help, courage, loyalty, compassion, wonder, and beauty.

  Louis celebrates these and touches our very souls to remind us how amazing we are and how great our potential. It is my great pleasure and privilege to illustrate his work, and I have integrated the work of many talented artists to help carry the messages to you.

  Louis and I share a desire to transport you, to inspire and help you realize your power to shine and create magic *Little Worlds* of your own.

Diane Woods
Illustrator

Introduction

I was looking at the derivation of the word, "Microcosm". It comes from two Greek words: mikros—small, and kosmos—world. Thus, the phrase small worlds or little worlds. I thought, isn't that wonderful. It was when I was beginning to write the book you are holding.

When I communicated with Diane Woods, the artist with whom I collaborate on my books, she understood this concept of "little worlds" instantly and began to make visual images of "little worlds" in her turn to accompany the poems.

As I continued to write the book, the poems formed into "little worlds" that expressed a hint or a trace of a larger world. However, I found that I did not have to go beyond the "little world" to communicate the larger world.

A crisp, clean tablecloth, a table set just so, a crystal vase filled with freshly cut Spring flowers was as far as I needed to go. The object itself or the tiny gesture or the subtle incline of the child's neck as he explained something to his Mama was enough.

The whole vast cosmos was in the Peach blossom pressed against the early morning window.

This is how the book came to be called *Little Worlds.* I invite you to enter these little worlds. May they inspire you to create your own little worlds.

It's very important to me that the words I use to communicate are understood. I advise the use of a dictionary. Additionally, there is a glossary at the back of the book with words that aren't that common.

Louis Alan Swartz
April 12, 2019
Los Angeles

I really want to hear from you.

I take great joy in hearing from my readers.

Any communication I receive on any subject will be answered. Here is my email address.

louisalanswartz@constructedofmagic.com

Little Worlds

I waken to a haunting melody
In a place where the Fairy Lanterns glow
Upon a meadow in the high country.
On blue hills above Mountain Lilacs grow.
This little world remembers to me
A gracious universe from long ago.

Chapter One

Spring

Amazement

Spring is coming again to the mountains.
I stand in awe, humbled and reverent.
High above fly giant, white Whooping Cranes.
Purple wild flowers are proud and silent.
I am struck by a sacred amazement.

Viewing the Iris

She viewed the Iris with an artist's eye.
The three standards* possessed a dignity.
It was as if painted with crimson dye.
The petals were soft, veined and feathery.
Ruffled red falls* drooped in harmony.
Somehow it bespoke immortality.

*Each Iris flower contains six petals.
Three of them stand straight up. These are
called the standards. The other three droop
downwards. These are the falls.

Letter

The desk was below the window
Which opened onto the east.
She sat bolt upright
In a straight-backed chair.

A carved glass vase of Daffodils
Atop her special wooden desk
In the pervasive quiet
Of an early Sunday morning.

She was startled
To almost hear a rustling
Behind her and just above,
Soundless and endearing.

She perceived a kindly
Presence reassuringly
Warm beside her,
Unobtrusively there.

Comforted and awed,
She returned to her letter,
"What do you say to a man
Who has lost this much?"

She completed the easy part.
"How is your back healing?"

"Did Bess come by?"
"How I have missed you."

But she was stymied
By that which she
Really wanted to say
To a man so bereft.

From the backyard
A Peachtree pressed
Pinkie, purple lavender
Blossoms on the window.

All she wished to say seemed
To be contained in the blossom.
Her words halted short of the image,
It was all there in the blossom.

The life she lived with him as a child.
Those long walks she took with him.
The last snow of a long cold Winter
Giving way to the early Spring.

"Daddy, do you remember the Crocuses
Of red, blue, violet and yellow
Pushing up through the late snow
Signaling yet another Spring?"

"And do you recall the old stone tower
Overgrown with unruly wild roses
Of deepest red and unexpected purple
We had never seen or imagined before?"

"I remember this, Daddy, as Spring has come
Once again to our treasured New England.
The old Peachtree has blossomed once again
Letting us know we are forever beautiful."

Enough

In my backyard a Cedar Tree.
Bluebird sings a Spring melody.
Somehow, this is enough for me.

Eastern Red Cedar

It's dawn! She's joyed at the gift of one more day.
Outside, she sees the Eastern Red Cedar tree
Standing reassuringly near the pathway,
Softening her present life's adversity,
Restoring her balance and tranquility.

Painter

Dedicated to Diane Woods

Before she could walk a step
Or had uttered her first word,
The perception of color
Thrilled her and caused her huge joy.

As a woman it was the same.
Spring was opening again.
It was for her ecstatic
And near unbearable.

She was unable to face
Overwhelming emotions
That Springtime always evoked,
Stirring sensitivities.

And so it was this morning.
Sun rose above the blue hills
Profuse with Mountain Lilacs.

As she walked the well-worn trail
From home to the wooden bridge,
Beyond the yellow Poppies
Covering the field below,
Beyond where she could now see,

She felt like all earth's beauty
And all the world's sorrow
Were contained within her heart
Insisting to be expressed.

She was experiencing
A full sensory overload
As always occurred in Spring
When the wildflowers came.

This Springtime she was in love,
Felt with almost no restraint.
She had not felt this ever
At any time in this lifetime.

Walking home along the stream
Swollen by the melting snow
She felt she was exploding
From the intense colors within.

That combined with the newly
Opened emotions of love
Flushed her face and made her cry.
It was too much all at once.

Reaching home she went straight
To her paints and set to work.
Relief began to set in
As she applied the yellows.

She painted as the sun set
And through the night to the sunrise
Until she was finally at peace
And able to take her rest.

Arched Wooden Bridge

Over the pond was an arched wooden bridge
That ended beside an aged Willow Tree.
Living on earth is a sacred privilege,
A joy to be part of humanity,
Sharing the hope of finally living free.
I will never find a finer family.

April, I Will Go

There is a meadow
In the high country.
Yellow flowers grow.
After winter's snow,
April, I will go.

Pasture

Behind the Willow began a steep trail
That wound its way through an old Oak forest
To a soft pasture from a fairytale.
From here the angel's realm could be accessed.
From here the distance there was the shortest.

Nature's Honesty

I went to Mendocino in Springtime
To a place where the Fairy Lanterns grow,
To realign the dreams of a lifetime
And unearth purposes from long ago.
I see Wild Irises of indigo.

The hillside is covered with Purple Sage.
These wildflowers wish to speak to me.
Feel quite giddy for a man of my age.
I can still be all that I've wished to be.
I'm overawed by nature's honesty.

Harmony

Earth is becoming increasingly dear to me.
Springtime has come to the northern woodland.
Bright, wild, red and pink Roses I can see,
Entwine the hill above where I stand
Beside the green Maples noble and grand.

Migratory birds are now returning
To their familiar homes here in the north.
By the lakeside Wild Geese are walking.
It's my eightieth birthday, May the fourth.
A future of joy's mine as I walk forth.

Going to be All Right

New England early Spring
Just after a cold spell.
Pale green buds opening.
The sunrise wishes me well.
Dawn has a tale to tell.

I'm happy here on Earth.
Once again, I perceive
The miracle of birth.
Someday I'll take my leave,
One more life to achieve.

But for now it is Spring.
I'm still standing upright.
Each day I learn something
And walk in the sunlight.
Going to be all right.

Chapter Two

Aesthetics

Aesthetic

Wakened to a haunting melody
Familiar to me yet from long ago.
Heard an otherworldly harmony.
Saw the colors of a unique rainbow,
An aesthetic universe's shadow.

A Place

Perhaps, you may have had a perception,
An almost overwhelmingly delicious feeling
That there was a whole wondrous realm
Inside of you or around you or part of you.
You reach it for a fleeting moment and then
It appears to be gone, but you know it isn't.

In this holy place tears of joy flow freely
And communion is intensely experienced.
Here it is possible to receive and perceive
An aesthetic inexpressible in human words.
Colors exist here unknown on this earth,
Sounds not heard here for a thousand years.

This is a place to which you can be transported.
The means of conveyance are stately and elegant.
You can hear laughter echoing from the sky.
It's somewhere right next to you or just behind.
But in actual truth it is not, in fact, located at all.
It has forever been sitting right next to you all along.

Magic

Your own imaginary universe
Is much realer than is the real one.
Divine imagination can traverse
Countless worlds when all is said and done.
This magic can be attained by anyone.

I've Decided to Begin Anew

By myself at home on a Sunday.
It is the way it has been of late.
My passion for life seems faraway.
Pink roses climb on the garden gate.
Somehow, I've lost my will to create.

Scarlet, vermilion, peacock blue,
We lived inside a lovely rainbow.
Every color reminds me of you
Though you took your leave so long ago.
You were all the joy a girl could know.

I never lost my ability.
I've decided to begin anew.
My watercolors are before me.
First, I apply a wash of light blue.
The painting alone will see me through.

The Painter and the Fairy

For Diane and Ingrid

The painter lived only to make beauty,
Just beauty with no other rationale.

In early dawn, there arrived a fairy.
The fairy's words were soft and whimsical,
"I came to impart some magic to thee,"
Her tone was caring and instructional,
"From the land of ultimate harmony."
Her voice was clear and yet, ethereal.

"I know for certain you expected me.
A long time I've watched you paint from afar.
I'm here to help you with your artistry.
I traveled here upon a falling star.
Magic truly is not a mystery."
She handed her a glowing crystal jar,
"It's filled with concentrated ecstasy."

"Take it in your hand, it is a gift from me.
It contains fairy dust, rainbows and things.
It is yours to use with audacity.
With it you can change what tomorrow brings.
It's a gift through you to humanity.
With it paint the world gloriously."

Blue Iris

She had lost touch with her own beauty,
Her personal willingness to create.
Outside, blue Irises bloomed gorgeously.
She walked down the path through the garden gate.
She perceived a deep blue bloom lovingly,
Felt her own artistry rejuvenate.

A Painter

Blue Lilacs beyond the garden gate
Opened an image of eternity.
She cherished the freedom to create
Forms reflecting nature's harmony.

Beauty

Primary is the unique aesthetic
Each individual brings to this earth.
Each soul is natively artistic.
The beauty we create measures our worth.
A new wonder comes with each human birth.

Artist

A girl born with a passion to create.
To life's touch she was ultra-receptive.
Was our goodness she worked to celebrate.
She was utterly beyond sensitive.
Without making beauty she couldn't live.

Aspen Stand

This stand of Aspens has lived near this stream
For much more than ten thousand of Earth's years.
I remember seeing them in a dream
Turned full on yellow as Winter nears.
Leaves flutter in light breeze as the mist clears.

There's a calmness I feel before these trees,
A reassurance I'm necessary
As is every leaf quaking in the breeze.
Hear the whisper of the forest fairy
Softly in the ancient sanctuary.

She tells of a natural harmony.
The trunk of the Aspen is strong and straight,
But bends in the Autumn wind gracefully.
Can see the future if I concentrate.
Eternity is now. I need not wait.

24

Let Me Return Again

To attempt to communicate
That which has always been
Right there in the open.
Wanting somehow to speak
To the spiritually deaf.
Senses chemically dulled,
Made unresponsive
By the toll taken
By the lies heard
Over countless lifetimes.
They have almost completely
Lost the ability to hear.

Unwilling and jaded
They are living
In a manufactured
World ubiquitously
There to consume.
They've relinquished
Their right of creation.
Instead receiving willingly
A readymade world,
Slick and sexy,
That requires only
That they push play.

Long, long ago
When we lived
In the mountains
We would play
And sing our songs.
I remember
An old man
With wobbly legs,
Who yet could play
His fiddle late
Into the night
Weaving melodies
Out of the air.

We would spin verses
Right there on the spot.
Grandma, blind in one eye,
Half sighted in the other,
Sang in forgotten tongue,
Hoisted her heart
Into the harmony.
Now and then
A stranger would
Join into the music,
Would be welcomed,
Fed and housed.
He may bring
Verses and melodies
From other places
Telling tales of wars
And migrations,

Remembrance
Of unlikely heroes
Who had stood up
And stood firm
When others faltered.

These songs were woven
In the cloth of our lives.
Grandma tapped the rhythm
With a handmade shoe.
In the kitchen were the smells
Of home grown spices,
Her stew simmering
On her wood fired stove.
There were stories and songs
Of gentle creatures
Who once walked here
And who will come again.

Give me the chance
To return once again
To those happy times
When we could play
With our own hands,
Sing with our voices.
Any person living
Was able to create
His very own verses
Telling personal stories
Of his losses, triumphs,
His sadness and dreams.
Let me return again.

Found Poem

(I found this "poem" in "The Color Dictionary Of Flowers and Plants". I present it here just as it was written in the dictionary.)

"This is one of the showiest of Orchids, but it is also one of the most difficult to grow successfully.

For the most part the plants are found high in the mountains of Mexico, where they are daily bathed in mist and where the temp. is nearly constant.

In the greenhouse a constant temp. Summer and Winter of sixty degrees Fahrenheit should be aimed at, although lower readings are permissible in the Winter, and the atmosphere should be moist and buoyant.

Hot, dry conditions are resented by the plants and if persisted in for too long may be lethal."

Sarah

When Sarah died in nineteen twenty-three
Ten thousand people lined the boulevard
Watching the caisson pass, reverently.
The actress was admired and adored.
She could touch an aesthetic harmony.
They came to say, "We'll miss you, mon amie."

*Sarah Bernhardt (1843 to 1923) An astounding
French actress who had the ability to communicate
directly to the members of the audience on a spiritual
level aesthetically.*

The Strength to Imagine

Your own create is genuine.
Retain the strength to imagine.

Majesty

Appreciate each person's magnificence,
Each expression of personal artistry.
Treated with kindness, tolerance and patience,
They begin to discover their brilliancy,
Their unique individual majesty.

If It's Worth Doing

In both living and art I have come to see
If something is worth doing at all,
It is worth doing with grace and beauty.

Aesthetic of Kindness

I perceived the aesthetic of kindness
In a selfless gesture of charity.
The child was alone and country less.
With unconditional humanity,
She took the lost child home graciously
And warmly welcomed her courteously.

Storm

The heaving night sea was lit by lightning.
Flocks of sea birds, startled by the thunder,
Took to the sky as night was darkening.
Could see giant, old trees blown asunder.
I was trembling and possessed by wonder.

Mountains that Rise
from the Sea

You're giant mountains that rise from the sea.
You're something of near ultimate beauty.

Mozart

There is something about his music
That quiets the soul immeasurably.

Chapter Three

Marriage, Family, Children

My Wife

In the vase Wild Roses and Queen Anne's Lace
She placed on the kitchen table just so.
Wonder perceived in the commonplace.
Aesthetic recalled from long ago.
Profound tenderness continues to grow.

Swan

Mother and daughter walking hand in hand
Beside a small pond, peaceful and silent,
When they saw a great Swan gracefully land.
Overcome with awe and astonishment,
They held each other in shared wonderment.

All the Woman

You're all the woman you've ever been
And you are able to love again.

With Child

Grace told me she was able to perceive
The world through a brand-new pair of eyes,
That her life had begun to interweave
With her child's life and to harmonize
In loving, spontaneous lullabies.

Lullaby

She was downstairs folding the week's laundry
Remembering things so hard to express.
She was protesting living's brevity.
She still had seven or eight shirts to press.
Loss of purpose had left her spiritless.

Sound of a flute through a window nearby
Awakened an aesthetic memory
When she fell asleep to a lullaby
Sung to her by her mother lovingly.
Caused her, again, to view life hopefully.

Astonishment

My time with the child at dawn was blessed.
I was enraptured by a wonderment.
The rising and falling of his small chest.
He gave me spiritual nourishment,
An uncontainable astonishment.

Ginger Jar

At the first landing of the back stair
On a wooden stand was a ginger jar,
Burnished gold as if by an angel's hair.
At the top was a glowing morning star.
I knew not by what chance it ended there.
At peace as a boy with the ginger jar.

Communication

The child possessed grace and dignity,
But lived in a universe of his own.
The teacher perceived his ability
And the sensitivity he had shown,
But could not reach him to any degree.

The child had never uttered a sound,
But drew creatures on a pad endlessly.
The teacher saw them as he came around.
He knelt down beside him courteously.
With his pen he drew a creature artfully.
The boy responded with hilarity.
From then on the boy got on splendidly.

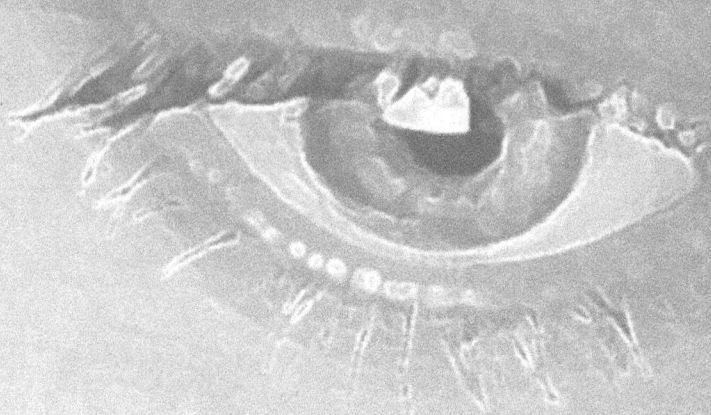

Comfort

Next door I could hear my mother crying.
It was just before I was to turn three.
She was not aware I was listening.
She entered my room unexpectedly
And she lovingly laid down beside me.

Schmo

She'd made the bed with an extra crispness.
Her note said, "I love you but I had to go."
Her leaving was caused by my thoughtlessness.
Saw this coming so very long ago.
My thoughts were so utterly comfortless.
I'm responsible for being a schmo.
I can still make this right nevertheless.

Being Enough

She was an unwilling passenger
Living with a man who wanted more.
For him she was never enough.
He wanted someone to die for.
She wished to live in harmony
With a man possessed of courtesy
Who would take her as she was
And let her be as she wished to be.

"I appreciate your willingness to listen.
Living alone these years has been rough.
At long last my heart begins to open.
The great relief of being able to be enough."

Remembrance of a
State of Grace

There is beauty in the ocean
As I walk across the sand.
Passions and purposes
Intimate and grand.

Anchored in benevolence
As I hold my child's hand
Perception of innocence
Sea birds in the tideland.

Cool sand between my toes.
I have a brief and tiny inkling
Of what the child sees and knows.
Can hear the lovely sea birds sing.

Memory of ancient journey
Far into light years of space.
I try to read the answers
In my boy child's face.

There may be a divine plan
Lost in unremembered eons
For midgets, giants and man
Seen in another planet's dawns.

Walking in September sand
Autumn's chill feel on my face
With my child hand in hand
Recall another time and place
Remembrance of a state of grace.

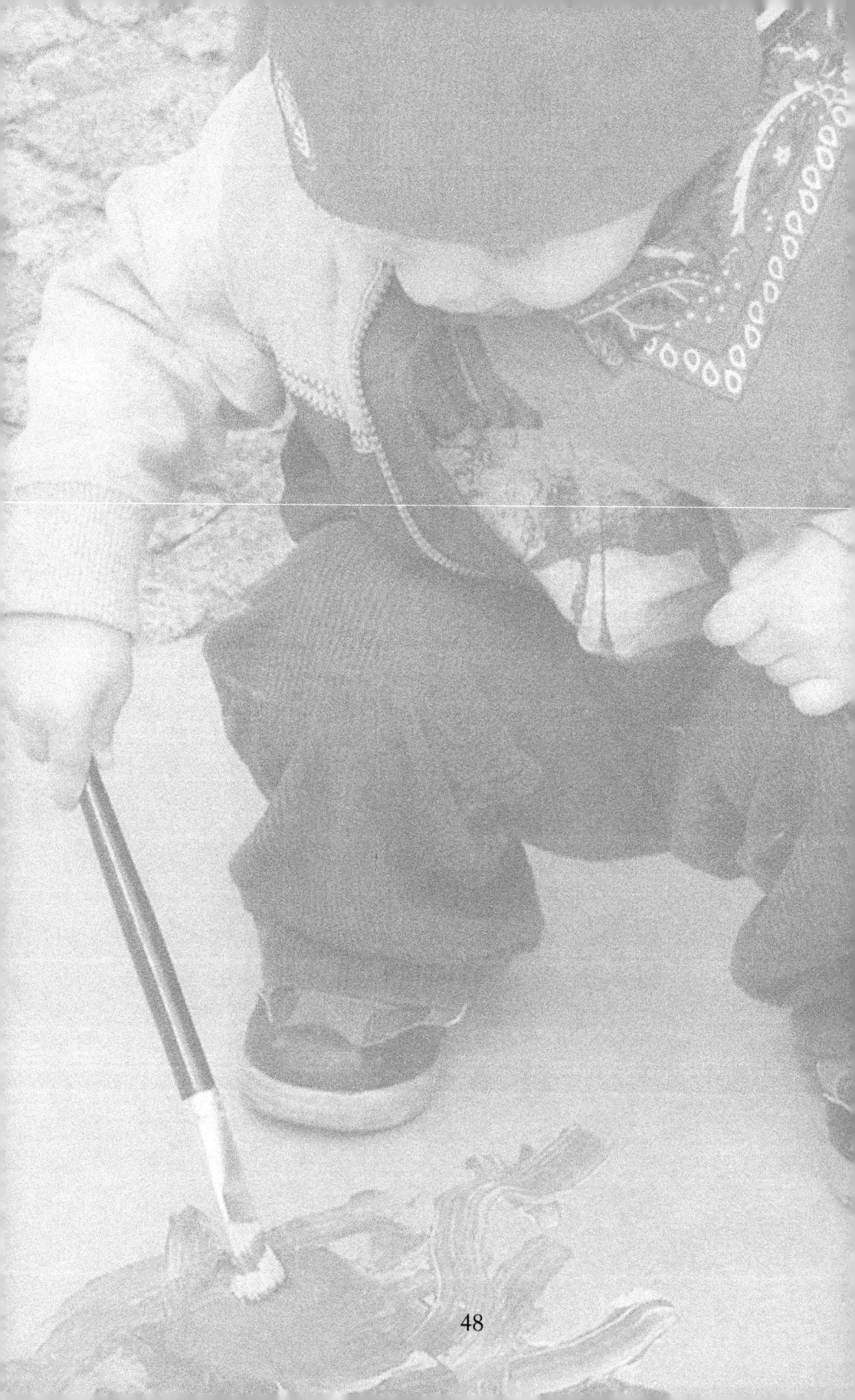

Child's Imagination

There's nothing as joyously
Unrestrained and wild
As the unfettered imagination
Of a child.

Teaching a Child

In teaching a child validate
His personal and unique vision,
His own ability to create.

Tiny Chair

I knelt down to see what the boy had found.
I sat beside him on a tiny chair.
It's the little things that often astound.
So much a daddy and child can share.
With him I was able to be aware
Of marvels surrounding us everywhere.

Pride

My son painted a picture for me,
Sun and planets in a field of blue.
I ask how proud can a father be?
Felt utter elation through and through.
Such beauty made by a boy of two.

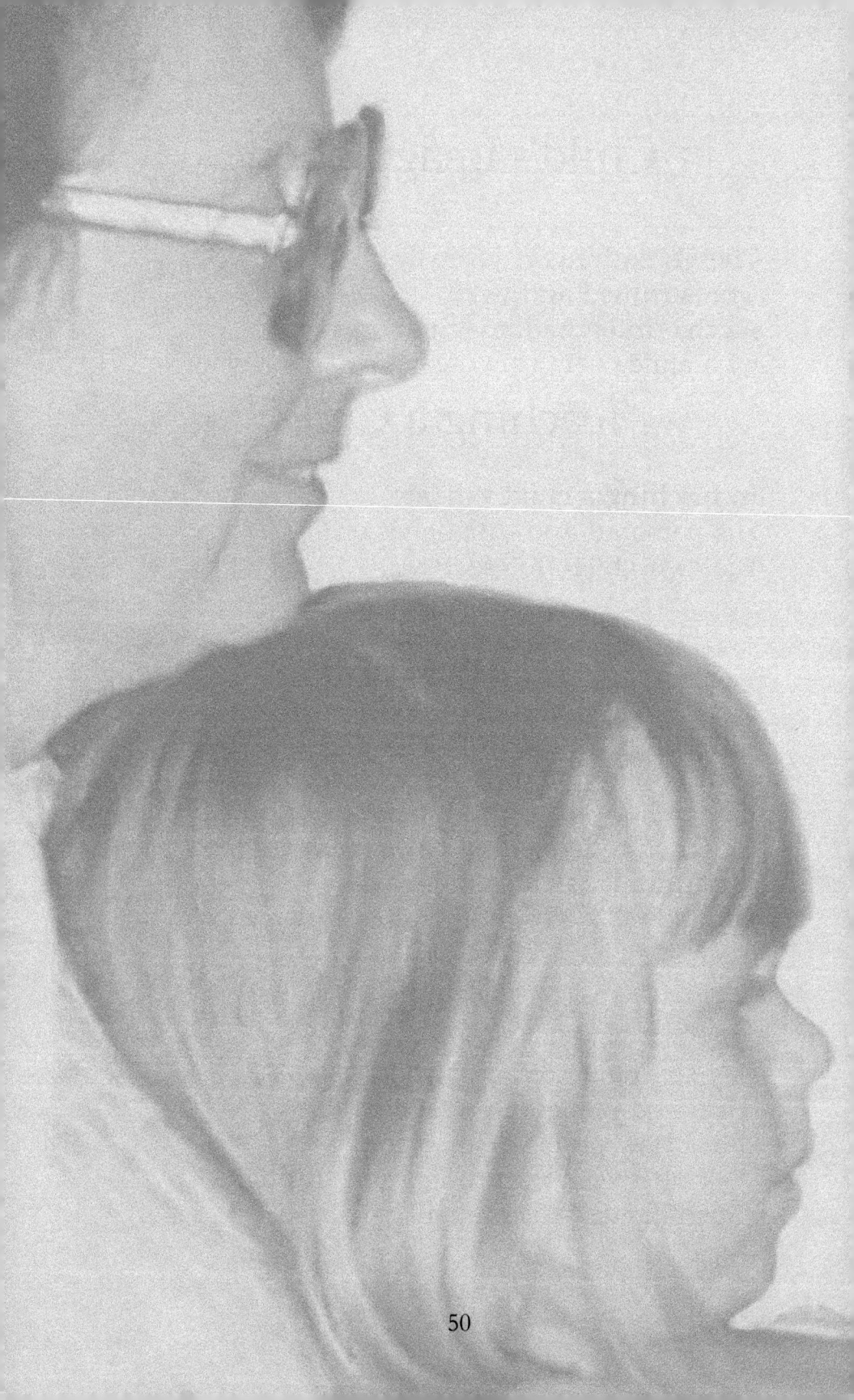

Teacher

A teacher I recall with great fondness.
Was the first person to believe in me.
She possessed a steadfast constructiveness.
It was her enormous expectancy
That opened the best in me constantly.

Learning

The teacher patiently
Teaching us to read
Enabling us to comprehend
Page by page.
My young hours in her class
Nourished a seed.
As I grew I learned
The beauty of the language.
Knew not the wonders
This learning
Would presage.

Children

Respecting each child's right to create
Is the highest level of sanity.
Permit each child to articulate
His personal viewpoint of reality.
Venerate his innocent honesty.
Such children will free us ultimately.

Wife

I appreciate all the times you've gone
Way out of your way for each one of us.
Admire how you keep on carrying on.
You're nothing short of miraculous.
All of this and you're also hilarious.

Little things handled seen and unseen.
Consciously creating such happiness.
The always understanding ear you've been.
I so respect your daily courageousness.
One hell of a marriage with which we're blessed.

Anticipated needs graciously filled.
A well-made bed, laundry fresh and clean.
It's a lovely thing we've been able to build.
It's so easy to treat you like a queen.
You have no idea how much help you've been.

I'm quite ready to do it all again
In some future time in another place.
A long, long time from now I imagine.
Where we'll meet each other face to face.
I will be able to perceive your grace.

Notes She Left Me

There's homemade meatloaf in the frig.
(Better cold than heated I think.)
Frank has a fever.
(Probably misses his sister.)
He's getting better.
There's some day-old cornbread.
(But it's good.)
God! I love you so much!
It's OK to wake me.

———————

I'm really sorry about last night.
There's a blueberry pie on the top shelf.
Don't know what gets into me sometimes.

———————

There's some leftover tuna casserole.
I think it's pretty good.
This war is really getting to me.
Senseless—so utterly senseless.
The sprinkler nearest the porch is broken.
See what you can do.

Joy

The smell of hot spiced tea with cinnamon.
Another Spring morning to celebrate.
Kitchen lit up by the rising sun.
My wife is standing at the garden gate.
A joy not easy to communicate.

Our Marriage

To find and draw out the magnificence
That each of us inherently possess,
The acknowledgement of shared wonderments,
Engendered by a certain selflessness,
Is the key to our marriage's success.

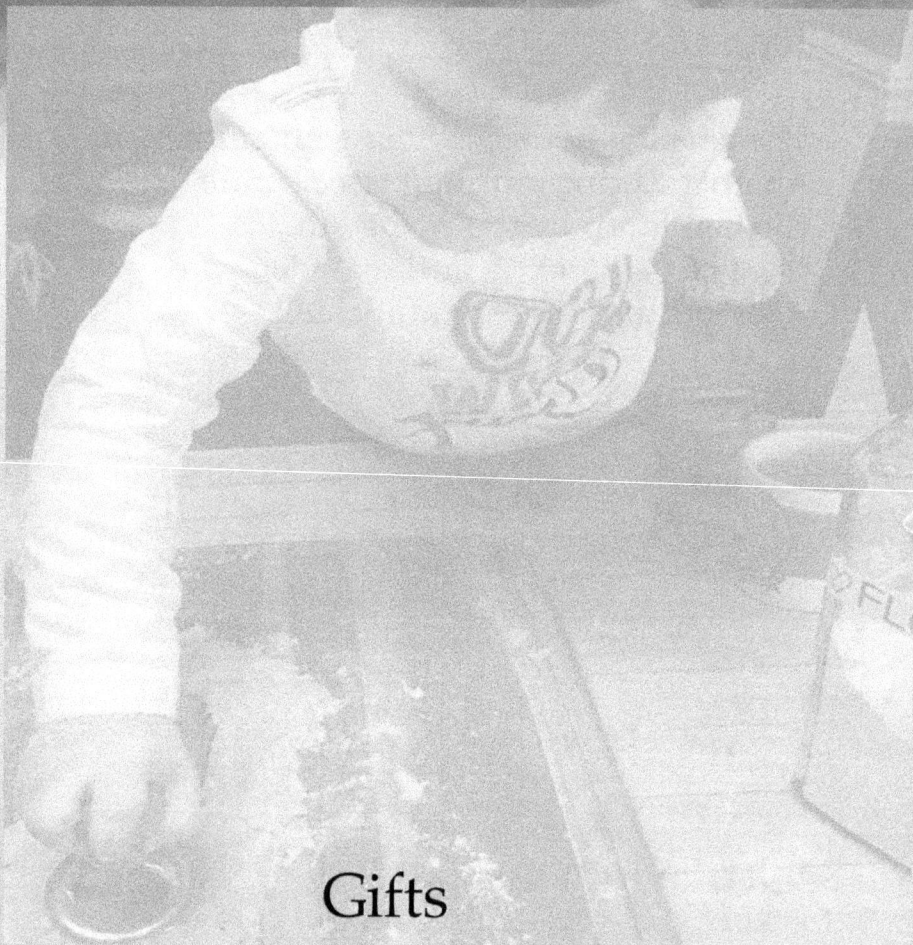

Gifts

You are the little presents to your wife.
You teach your child the good things of life.

In the Park with Daddy

My childhood years were blessed.
Park a mile away.
There I was happiest
With my dad on Sunday.

There was a boat we made,
Miniature sailing ship,
Carved from wood with my blade
Proud flag at the sail's tip.

On the pond I would sail,
The Captain of the Sea.
Recall this in detail,
In the park with Daddy.

Remembrance of Childhood's Time

Silvery outlines of celebratory streamers.
Uncontainable exuberance experienced.
Early summer's full on joy of family.
Children's giddy and delighted screams.
Drenched in a sudden summer shower.
Glades found filled with enchantment.
Benevolent creatures roamed the forest.
There were angels in the peach orchard.
We heard laughter among the flowers.
Diamonds lit up the evening sky.
Remembrance of childhood's time.

Chapter Four

Humanity

Milestones

It's the tiny increments of kindness
That are the milestones of human progress.

The Most in Their Hearts

The most trouble
We get into is
Trying to possess
That which we
Already own.

Some of the happiest
People I know
Have the least
In their name
And the most
In their hearts.

Our Hope

We have the ability to contemplate:
An end to ignorance's tyranny,
The complete cessation of human hate,
Recovering our sensitivity
To the needs of all humanity,
The return of pervasive sanity.

Age of Kindness

Cause this to be the age of kindness.
It needs a responsive and heroic heart
And all of the understanding we possess.
Caring for our fellows is s fine art.
There's no time like right now to start.

Thread

There is an inkling, a spark and a golden thread
Woven through the fabric of human history,
An immortal awareness we've inherited.

Woven

Goodness is woven
Into the fabric
Of our existence.

Kind

Mankind is by nature innately kind.
We are inherently aesthetic.
This appears to be how we are designed.
It is basic to our human fabric.
It's how an actual person is defined.

Choice

Some things we're unable to legislate
Such as love and responsibility.
By his own choice a man's considerate.
You can't order or enforce empathy.
These virtues are created personally.

Opportunity

In the land, I sense a disquietude.
Yet, it's a time of opportunity.
We need a vast change in our attitude.
If we work for real justice doggedly
And stand firm in the face of tyranny,
We'll redirect our future history.

Respect

There is a depth of respect appropriate
For each living person in the universe.
If we all, from right now, were to dedicate
Our wisdom, love, courage and strength to reverse
The downward spiral of disrespect and hate
And if we all began to communicate,
We could change our future before it's too late.

Free

The Old Man's example helped me realize
Love of man engenders a decency.
It awakens purpose and clarifies
Mankind's fundamental reason to be:
To help all of his brothers to live free.

Justice

It is in the daily continuance
That the actual heroism lies.
The man who shows up has a fighting chance.
He who carries on without compromise,
Will live to see the sun of justice rise.

Message

*Iris is the Greek Goddess of the Rainbow.
She was the messenger of the gods. She is
said to travel on a rainbow while carrying
messages from the gods to mortals. Iris links
the gods to humanity. She travels with the
speed of the wind from one end of the world
to the other. She is a divine messenger.*

Goddess of the message and the rainbow
Arrived here urgently in a fury.

"I have a message humankind must know,
I came here to avert a catastrophe,
To help restore human harmony.

"I crossed the divide between Earth and Heaven
To tell the people what the gods have known.
For some time Earth has been in a tailspin.
This planet is fast becoming a war zone.
The seeds of hatred need to be unsown.

"Man needs to restore his native kindness.
Every human being has the right to live.
Men need to recover their gentleness
And regain the courage to forgive.
A change of viewpoint is imperative."

Tell Him

When a man feels he can no longer assist
And his contributions lack worth and value,
When he thinks his absence wouldn't be missed,
That he doesn't matter, although untrue,
At that very point he will cease to exist.
Tell him he matters and his work has virtue.
You will be amazed at what he now can do.

May You Always Remember

May you always remember
The spiritual courtesies
That are native to our kind
And may you live by them.

A stranger crosses your path.
He wears strange worn shoes.
He speaks a foreign tongue.
He seems worried and lost.

Offer him sanctuary.
Give him water, feed him.
Bring him in from the cold.
Welcome him to your home.

Each living human soul
Possesses personal goodness.
Respect his inborn right
To walk upon this earth.

May you always remember
The spiritual courtesies
That are native to our kind
And may you live by them.

Captain

He was a gentleman of the highest order
Who practiced an honest courtesy.
Never met a person who was friendlier.
He possessed a natural gentility.
His presence on board made our work easier.
He led us with a firm sensitivity
That inspired an unreserved constancy
And released for us terrific ability.

Mercy

He was looking for some small humanness
On the road as a rootless refugee.
Nearing a point of utter hopelessness,
He witnessed an act of selfless mercy,
Warm bowl of soup offered with courtesy.

The Greater Kindness

Our prime value is in our goodness.
Always pursue the greater kindness.

Humane

Definition of Humane,
Noah Webster's 1828 Dictionary
Having the feelings and dispositions proper
to man; having tenderness, compassion and
a disposition to treat others with kindness;
particularly in relieving them when in distress,
or in captivity, when they are helpless or
defenseless; kind; benevolent.

The living searched vainly in the debris
For a trace of anything alive at all.
Rubble piled as far as we could see.
Grandma warmed orphaned children with her shawl.
The weary doctor eased the agony.
In morning men came, the bodies to haul.
They wrapped them in saffron cloth gently.
In the distance, a mournful prayer call.

Without Hatred

She held back thoughts of revenge and hatred
Standing before the ruins of her street.
She had grown so weary of the bloodshed.
A child crawled between slabs of concrete.
She was possessed by compassion replete
While his wounds she began to wash and treat.

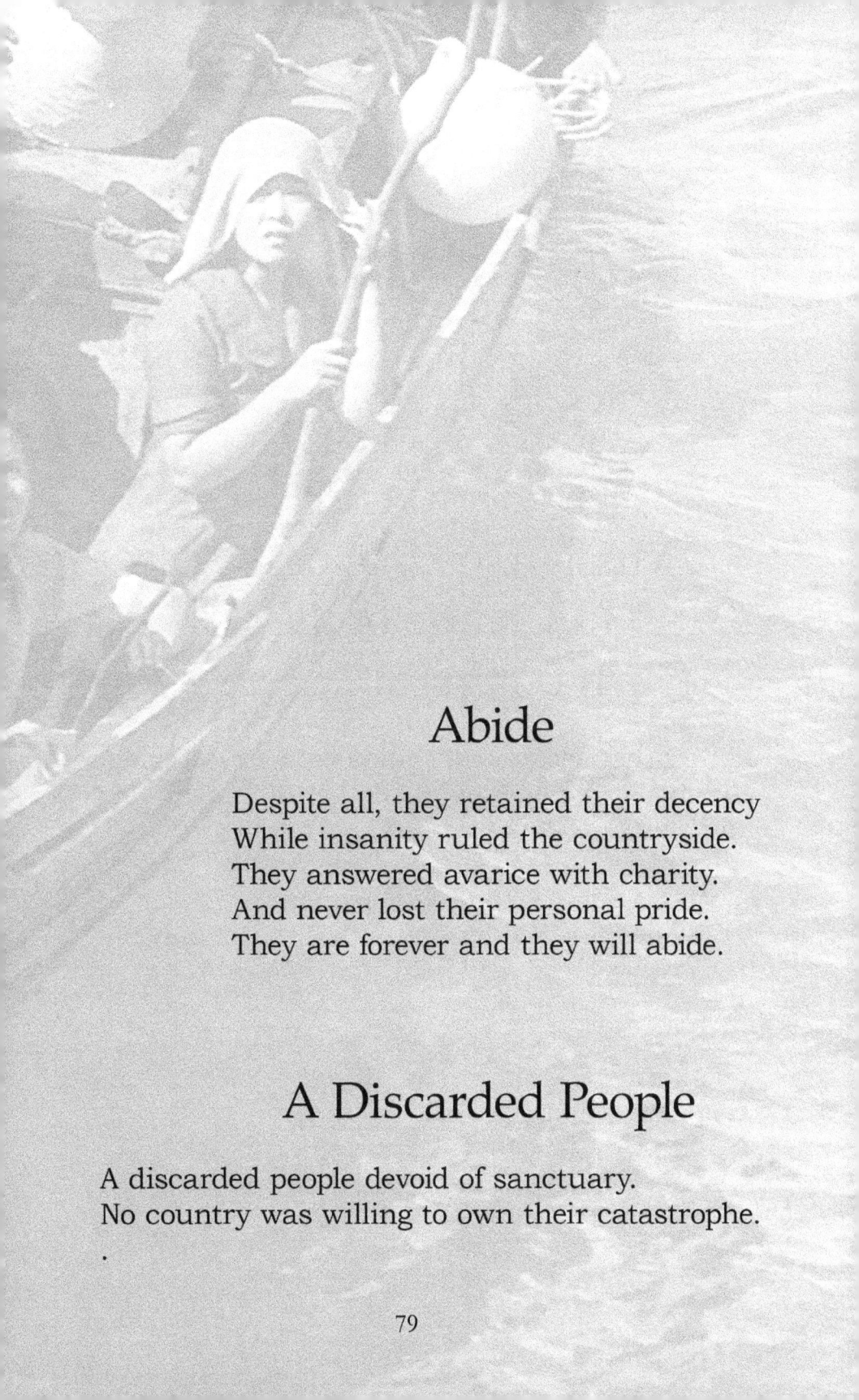

Abide

Despite all, they retained their decency
While insanity ruled the countryside.
They answered avarice with charity.
And never lost their personal pride.
They are forever and they will abide.

A Discarded People

A discarded people devoid of sanctuary.
No country was willing to own their catastrophe.
.

Excerpt from the Daily Mission Journal of the In Charge of the Earth Botanical Mission

I know that yesterday I commented on the enormous rudeness exhibited by the human inhabitants of this planet. Their manners are atrocious in the main. Some hold the viewpoint that certain of their races or ethnicities are inferior and/or are threatening in some way and deal with them as such.

They are heavily armed both personally with small arms and internationally with nuclear weapons designed for intraplanetary warfare. The fact that the use of a small fraction of such weapons would destroy their environment complete seems to escape them.

A major part of the populace appears to be almost devoid of any actual spiritual awareness. Harm is done with quasi religious justifications.

However, to be fair there are certain individuals and groups, while in the minority, who are highly aware spiritually and who are dedicated to bringing spiritual cognizance to Earth's inhabitants whatever it takes.

But, enough on that. It is not part of our mission orders and is only the behavior of one somewhat degraded Earth species.

On to much more important things. We have now cataloged and recorded 21,753 species of Orchids. These flowers (which I believe are completely unknown in our world) are absolutely magnificent. Earth has a wide variety of climates and topography. These flowers grow everywhere in the southern hemisphere. They are found from the high mountain country to deep in the hot rain forests. (Especially where the human species has not destroyed their habitat—a particularly irksome trait of the human species.)

These Orchids were created solely and only to be aesthetic and aesthetic they are. They are made of every imaginable color. There are reds and oranges that literally increase the speed of your blood flow just viewing them. Next, there is a full range of purples from the deepest, veined red purple to the softest and quietest light, light blue lavender and pink lavender.

The shapes and the forms exude an ineffable loveliness that evokes a desire to pray. But these shapes and forms seem incongruous in this earthly environment. (As if they did not belong here.) I am researching this.

The key questions are:

1. Who made them?

2. How did they get here?

3. What was the purpose of making 21,000 plus species?

4. Who was it that had the art, patience and desire to create them?

5. Where have their creators gone?

6. Did they just create them and leave? Unlikely.

I wonder. I am working on this. Thus far, this is the most important thing I have encountered on this spiritual desert of a planet.

I miss home. I miss the graciousness of my people, their manners suffused with respect and tolerance for all of their fellows. I miss walking the blessed ground that speaks to me in sacred and ancient tongues.

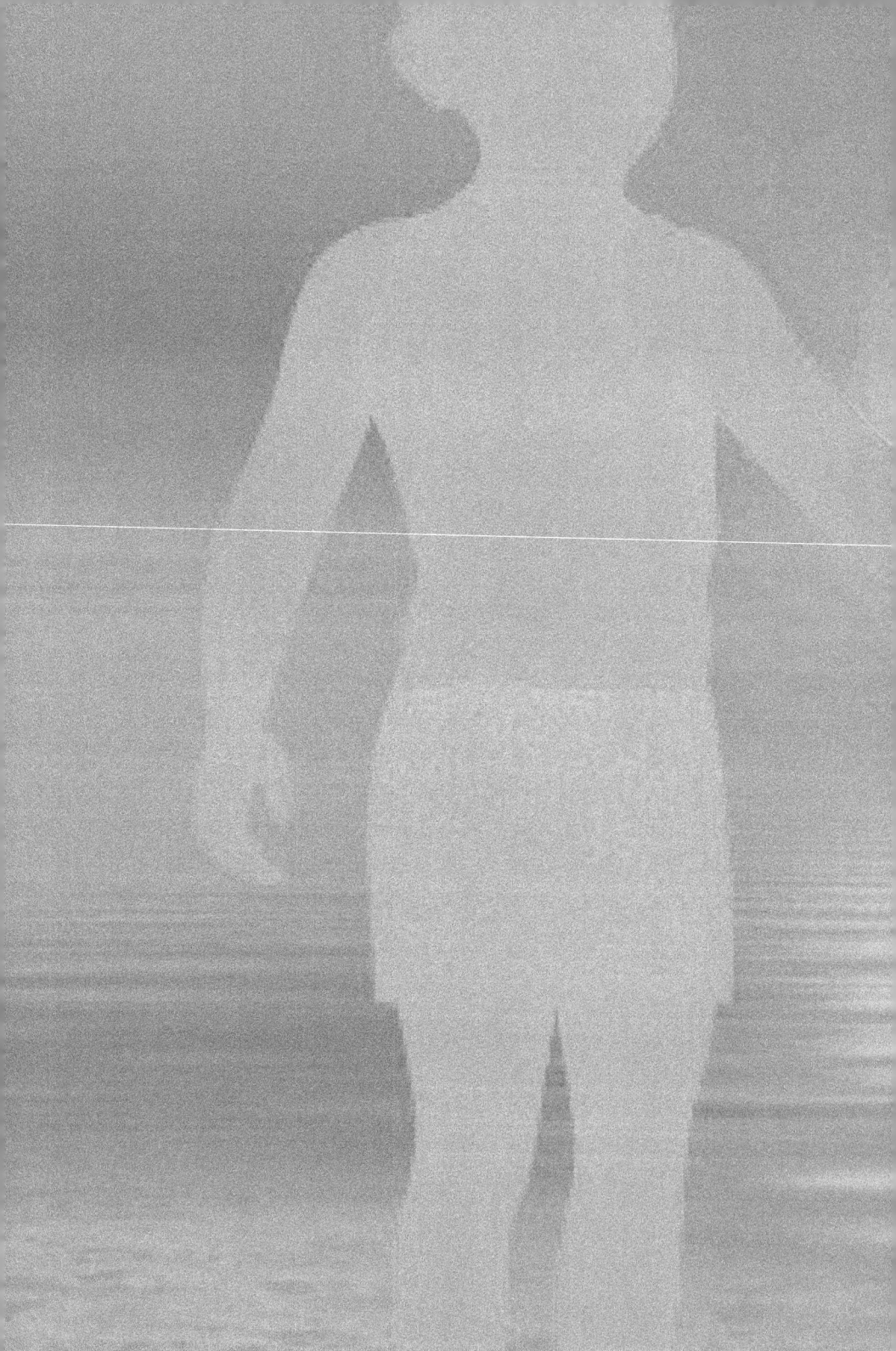

84

Home

Two children alone beneath the night sky.
Their faces spoke of endured tragedy.
Crimes against life one cannot justify
Destroyed their village and forced them to flee.
Their journey was devoid of decency.

An old couple, heading home, happened by.
They offered them a lift courteously.
They took them to their home which was nearby.
They gave them food which they ate hungrily.
Watching them the old man laughed joyfully
And said, "My dear, we've got some company."

Chapter 5

America

Inclusion

The spiritual commonality
Shared by each living soul on this planet
Is the truth beneath our equality,
A fundamental we must not forget.
Exclusion is the worst cruelty.
Inclusion is the soul of harmony.

America, My Country # 5

America, my country, I begin you again.
It was there in the original Declaration
Jefferson wrote on Market in Philly with Franklin
When they created the very basis of our Nation.

"All men are created equal..." they were to state,
The possibility each living man could live free.
With these five short words they opened liberty's floodgate
And struck a blow to a thousand years of tyranny.

Jefferson was, in actual fact, an idealist.
He was truly compassionate, extremely kind.
He did not, in fact, see the women and slaves he missed.
More than half of America was left far behind.

In spite of these flagrant omissions, this was the dawn
Of complete transformation in the affairs of man.
The truths from which this noble document was written
Are vital to the construct of an American.

Two hundred years later we're trying to comprehend
These five words, straightforward and plain,
To fully grasp the intention of the words they penned,
The open, unreserved, humanity they contain.

America, my country, I begin you again.
We have the capacity to achieve their intent
Letting these men know what they did wasn't done in vain.
Delivering equality to the full extent.

Peaceful Rebellion

*"I hold that a little rebellion now
and then is a good thing and as
necessary in the political world
as storms in the physical."*

*Thomas Jefferson Letter to James Madison
January 30th, 1787*

I begin to see a peaceful spirit
Of rebellion just now awakening
In our land and refusing to quit.
Out in the streets, the people are marching,
Their strident voices are again rising.
Bless the positive change they're here to bring.

The Eyes of Liberty

We can see the light in the eyes of Liberty.
We're willing to die rather than compromise
Our Divinely endowed right to live free.
.

Goodness

I believe there is a spark of goodness
Inborn, innate with each daughter and son,
That is integral to our humanness.
I looked for any guile. There was none.
This is vital to our happiness.

Democracy

There are certain things I'm able to see.
For their freedom, men can't be told to wait.
Essential to leadership, is mercy.
If we hustle, it's not too late
To restore actual democracy.

America, My Country # 6

(Imaginary letter from Peg Odem
of Boston to Margaret Spencer
of Philadelphia.)

7 June 1776

Dear Margaret,

Summer is blossoming everywhere. Every last seed and bulb I planted in my garden is blooming full on.

You should hear the talk here. Strong words spoken in the street about revolution and war. There is something else that has caught my interest like nothing else in my entire life.

There's a lot of talk about benevolence and equality. I haven't really grasped it all. Betsy Rowen was talking to me about a story she heard. A gentleman had been thrown from his horse on a country road far from town. He was hurt bad with a deep cut on his leg. A negro boy not even five saw it. He ran to the man—took his little shirt off and wrapped it tight around the leg to stem the bleeding. At the same time he hollered as loud as he could for help.

Betsy told me there was wonderful talk about this story. The people spoke about how there really seemed to be a spark of goodness in each person. Something...something spiritual or divine. I'm still trying to understand, but somehow it makes a lot of sense to me. They talked about how neither age, experience, education, cultivation or station in life mattered. This was inborn. There was something, somehow in them that would naturally cause them to do the right thing.

The idea was that this special sense of compassion was not limited to a noble few. This was a quality that came from the very heavens and was possessed by each and every man, woman and child.

This is such a magical thing. I can hardly get my wits around it. What a wonder this is. The idea that there is a native kindness in every person. And even beyond that—a spirit— some kind of spirit common to all people. Oh, Margaret, it takes my breath away.

The tomatoes are ripe and huge. I'm going to make a lovely salad for dinner tonight. I hope all is well with you and Sam and the children.

The Very Best,
Peg

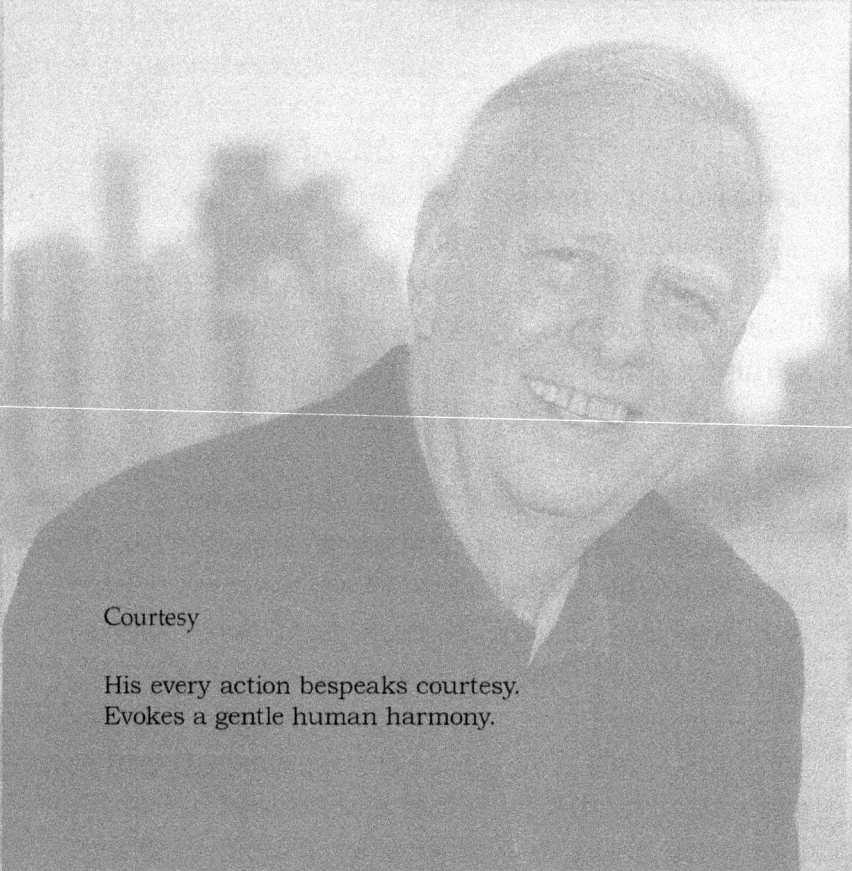

Courtesy

His every action bespeaks courtesy.
Evokes a gentle human harmony.

Dawn

Blue morning glories, soft and delicate
Opening beyond my window at dawn.
If justice comes not today, I can wait.
A few feet away, quietly a fawn.
I know how much we are depended on.

Compassion, respect and benevolence
Soften the hard edge of continuance.
Our children play outside in innocence.
It's our duty to give them a fair chance.
Freedom is not achieved by happenstance.

Chapter Six

The Human Spirit

Constructed of Goodness

The spirit is constructed of goodness.
He is on earth to engender beauty
And to alleviate human distress.
Belief in man without apology
Opens him to any possibility.

Miracle

Comprehend the miracle of a seed.
I knew a man who could heal with his hand.
The spirit has the power to intercede.
A boy jerked back from death by a command.
I must tell you I've seen these things first hand.
Allow me to show you another land.

Purpose

Intention in her face
Was warm and crystalline,
Loss and old age wasn't
Able to intervene.
Driven by purposes
Passionate and pristine,
Death hadn't the power
To decimate her dream.

Angels

Angels don't have wings but they do exist.
They walk among us with impunity.
Their only purpose here is to assist.
They are willing to get their hands dirty.
Ultimately, they are constructed of beauty.

They walk among us just like any man.
Some of them like beer and some like pizza.
But they are, in fact, much more than human.
Some enjoy sports, others like cinema,
They are unrecognized phenomena.

Possessing unconditional kindness,
Their presence engenders tranquility.
They're constantly helping with great finesse.
They draw out our love and humanity.
Hard to explain what their presence means to me.

I Think I am Going to be Fine

I went to a town in the north
Hoping to get my head straight.
It is here I am happiest.
I need time to be separate.
I think for now the noise can wait.

Lately I'm living day to day.
My world's soft and delicate.
Down the road's a quiet café.
Memories I wish to vacate.
Move myself to a kinder state.

I so needed to leave the scene.
I desired to disconnect.
To somehow reconstruct my dream
And be myself though not perfect,
Reestablish my self-respect.

I am not at all finished yet.
I think I'm going to be fine.
Sitting alone in the luncheonette
Street lit by a blue neon sign.
My world's beginning to align.

Mendocino

Dreams dreamt beneath the skies of Mendocino
Were so much realer than actuality.
In mid-summer when the hills turned yellow
Was a time of personal discovery.
Seeing the man into which I wished to grow.
Recalling Mendocino from long ago.

Visit to a Friend

It was in New Hampshire in early May,
My old friend and I beneath the window
In his stone kitchen, dawn on a Sunday.
I did not think my utter pain would show.
I was foolish to think he wouldn't know.

I had lost my personal confidence
And my belief in my own ability.
This and much more he was able to sense.
He perceived my strength and fragility.
Smiling at me he poured us some tea.

"I ask you please listen closely to me.
You are greater than you can imagine.
You have to live your life outrageously.
You have giant universes to win.
Denial of self is the greatest sin."

His words caused me to sit up, steel rod straight.
And made me cause without apology.
Life's purpose began to rejuvenate.
Felt a sudden rekindled fervency
To achieve my personal destiny.

Lilac Tree

To her seemed as though the war
Had lasted a thousand years.
She'd little left to live for,
Folding the laundry in tears.

Almost entered child's room,
Forgetting the catastrophe.
Absently picking up the broom,
Vainly sweeping at the debris.

In the back stood a Lilac Tree
In fragrant full purple bloom.
Beyond human agony,
Gave her hope life could resume.

There were birds in the blossoms
Singing in sweet harmony.
I still live whatever comes!
Heaven bless the Lilac Tree.

Extraordinary

The road to the extraordinary
Begins with fully living
In the ordinary.

Power

There is a depth of grace and willingness,
A raw spirit upon which we can draw
In moments of overwhelming distress,
When we are way beyond the final straw.
This is the finest power we possess.

Keep a Light On

Handle the practical
Responsibilities of life.
Attend to your duties
As a son, a father,
A brother and friend.
Run a proper household,
Take care of business.
But keep a light on
So that miracles
Can find you.

Walk Off

Good things seem
To happen to me
When there's two outs,
Bottom of the ninth.
We're down by one.
It's my turn to bat.
Forget the queasiness
In my stomach.
A man is on base.
A homer is required.
Much too quickly
We have a full count.
The third out
Isn't an option.
Afternoon sun
Is hot behind me.
Left field wall is
Distant, but clear.
Playing me deep.
The pitch comes.
Hangs in warm air
For seeming forever.
I swing as hard as I can.
Solid crack thrills me.
I know it is gone.

Courage

His ability to lose graciously,
The man's unrelenting courageousness,
Caused him to prevail through adversity.
When circumstances were the most hopeless,
He'd tap into some divine energy
And thus bring it all off ultimately.

There's So Much to Win

Outside my window
In early morning,
The patient Willow
Was saying something.
Could hear a bird sing.

Sweetness of the song
Softened my sorrow.
I need to be strong
To face tomorrow.
I know what I know.

I have not lost you.
You're all you have been
And I am still Lou.
It's time to begin.
There's so much to win.

Summer Sunset in Sonoma

"You have absolutely no idea
how good you are."

Said to him as the sun set
In late summer in Sonoma.
Said at a time when he'd
Lost grip on his wisdom.

With just those words he felt
A shift in how he saw
The earth on which he lived.
Before him was a stand of Elms.
He felt unreserved admiration
For these trees alone by the river.

It was a gift to see again
The grace and harmony
Contained in all living things.
There was laughter
In the warm summer grass.
Could now see a world around
Him infused with majesty.

Tapestry

Woven into the tapestry
Ancient tale to illuminate
Stitch by thoughtful stitch patiently
Hopeful world to recreate.

A time of human harmony,
A willingness to understand,
Openhearted help, courtesy,
Ingrained reverence for the land.

Sewing the colors one by one,
Recalled a time when we were free.
Earth was open to everyone.
Dreams sewn into the tapestry.

Where Do We Sleep Tonight?

May my ultimate legacy be
I retained my dignity and grace
In the face of utter insanity,
Anguish impossible to erase,
Annihilation of our birthplace.

Sifting through the rubble and debris
Objects of love and remembrance,
Toys of my children, Ben and Marie,
Broken China dishes, crushed house plants,
Doll fragments, shreds of boy's pants.

A mist of glass shards and masonry
Makes a rainbow of the morning light.
An aesthetic in the misery.
I cannot deal with moral or right,
It's only—where do we sleep tonight?

A Place I Wished for in a Dream

The child began his journey
To unknown and foreign places,
An unintended refugee.
Strange towns, unfamiliar faces,
Where homes had stood, empty spaces.

Memory of who had been lost,
Horror he'd seen with his own eyes,
Broken land he was forced to cross.
Look in his face when a man dies.
Planes approaching from western skies.

He crossed the desert to the sea.
By the roadside a friend had died.
Overcome by dark misery,
Standing by the ocean he cried.
In the warm sea wind his eyes dried.

"I need to find a place that's free,
A place where I've never been.
Possibly they would accept me."
Tender longings in the extreme.
"A place I wished for in a dream."

Sanctuary

Grandfather was surprised to be alive,
The block was flattened by artillery.
The rest of our family did not survive.
Neighbors lay before us in agony
Crushed by unfathomable cruelty.

The scene was utter horror incarnate.
We tended to the wounded desperately.
Some we helped. For many it was too late.
At one point Grandfather looked at me,
Was overwhelmed by the catastrophe.

Just after dawn some help finally arrived.
I could not explain this atrocity.
Grandpa held my hand and profusely cried.
There was no sense to this travesty.
In each other we found sanctuary.

Desert

The sunlit burnt gold desert plain
And the blue mountains beyond it,
Reminded her yet once again
She was forever a spirit.

Benevolence

Benevolence means to wish someone well.
Even the tattered old man in the street.
A faded war medal in his lapel.
Face hardened from living on the concrete.
His presence caused me to feel incomplete.

Somehow felt responsible for the guy.
Consider no living man second rate.
Able to hear his unspoken outcry.
To his life's agony, I could relate.
Our lives were not actually separate.

I gave him something to help him get by.
I took his worn hand and wished him Godspeed.
I could see a light come into his eye.
My meeting with him engendered a seed.
On a hopeful course, I could now proceed.

Wellspring

At its heart, the actual living
Of a life is a limitless wonder,
A sacred and divine wellspring.

Downpour

You are the downpour that ends the drought,
Sorrow and loss and carrying on.
Toughness, triumph and victory's shout.

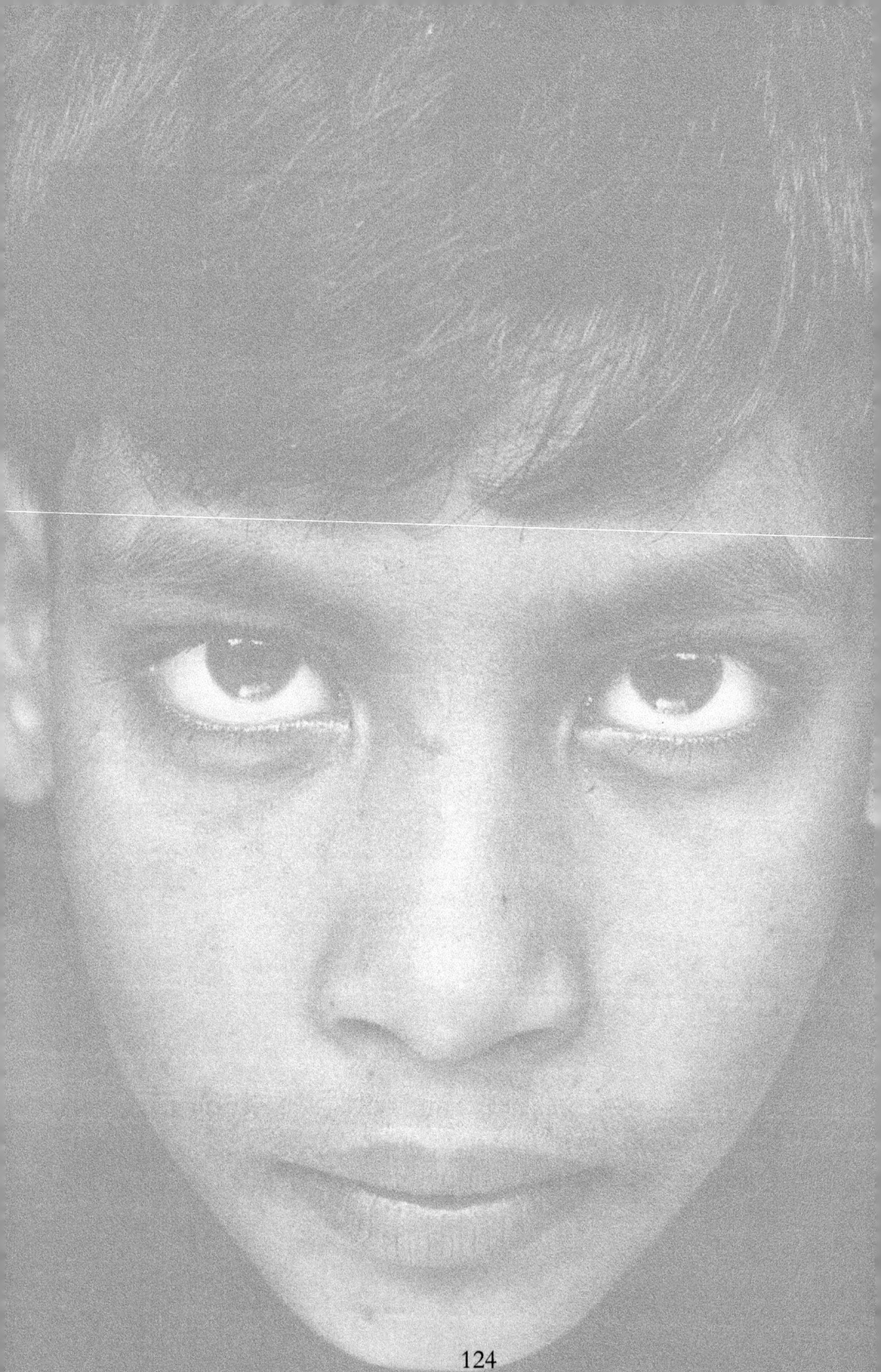

He Who Listens Ceaselessly

On a planet in a far distant galaxy
They gave each child a name appropriate
To his unique qualities and ability
And the good works he was destined to create.
This child's name:
He Who Listens Ceaselessly.

He grew to be a respected Officer.
In a time of worldwide catastrophe,
He was summoned by a noble messenger,
"We have urgent need for your diplomacy."
"What Sir, at this time, is required of me?"

"There are armed factions
At war on every side.
Your help's needed to avert calamity.
So much has been destroyed.
Many men have died.
Communication will restore sanity.
It needs a man who can listen ceaselessly."

He gathered the sides together one by one.
He listened to them with a fierce urgency.
He told them, "We'll be here until we're done."
And he proceeded to listen ceaselessly.

Empath

I remember him at the age of two,
Possessed of an absurd sensitivity.
Feeling what another felt through and
through,
Compassion laced with pure affinity,
Perceiving from another's point of view.
Able to love without apology.
These abilities strengthened as he grew.
I cannot describe in any degree
What knowing this child has meant to me.

Listen to the Ladies

Let us hear what the ladies have to say.
We have need of feminine sanity.
They always stand beside us come what may.
We require their grace and constancy.
They will surely take us out of harm's way.
Earth is healed by woman's humanity.

Wild Blueberries

I remember when they came
Fists pounding on the doors,
Ordering everyone into the street
Unfeeling horsemen with orders.

I remember earlier as a child
Gathering wild Blueberries
In wooden buckets for Grandma
Who made them into lovely pies.

I can remember selling the pies
Hot from the oven on the street
The smell of fresh cooked pie
Drew the people to me in droves.

I would have been happy forever
In those high mountain meadows
Until the big men came on horses
Pounding on our doors at dawn.

One day I will return once again
To those high mountain meadows,
Gather wild Blueberries in buckets
And bring them home to Grandma.

Subway

Confronting the work it takes to live free
On the Lexington Avenue Subway
In early Winter in New York City.
I believe what I believe come what may.
Holding fast to my purpose day by day.

To stay on a course and not deviate.
Required is a constant diligence.
The people on the train appear to wait
For a miraculous coincidence.
We cause our personal magnificence.

Displaced

We have walked almost halfway to somewhere.
We'll know where we're going when we get there,
Aware we are broken but we don't care.
Can smell something burning in the night air.
Our noble Flag is faded and threadbare.
We'll know where we're going when we get there.

Duty

The Captain was inspired by duty.
It was generated from the inside.
T'was reflected in the ship's company.
It manifested itself as real pride.
A man we're honored to serve alongside.

Care

He is possessed of an apparently
Unlimited willingness to be there
For us all through everything constantly.
Appreciate so his enduring care.
In his helping presence I can be free.

Humility

In greeting the old man he bowed his head.
My friend possessed a certain pridelessness.
With him human courtesy was inbred.
The joy of others was his happiness.
Granting other's greatness didn't make him less.
His profound strength came from his kindliness.

Greatness

His home was destroyed by artillary.
His niece and three daughters were killed inside.
Saw parts of his children in the debris.
His first thought was to put hatred aside.
Retained his love in the catastrophe.
Would not compromise his humanity.

Dr. Izzeldin Abuelaish, a Palestinian Doctor who healed both Israeli and Palestinian patients, had his house destroyed by Israeli tank fire in the 2009 Gaza War. His niece and three daughters were killed. In response, in 2010, he published a book entitled "I Shall Not Hate (A Gaza Doctor's Journey on the Road to Peace and Dignity).".

Worlds

There are wonders
Within your grasp.
There is magic
And imagination.

There is an intensity
Of passion possible.
There is humor
And rolling laughter,
Unrestrained hilarity.

There is fun
Just for fun
That goes so deep.
The utter stupendousness
Of human relationships.

There's a tenderness
And the profound
Comprehension
Of the worlds of others.
There is succor and help.

There is love
And behind the love
Is another level of love
And even yet
Another layer.

There is care
And greater care
And under that care
That does not end.

And compassion as well
And beneath it
There's compassion
Without condition.

There are corners
And crevices
And cubbies.
Places to look
And to listen.
Places in the heart
And also places
In the hearts of others
Where one can go.

There are infinite colors,
Forms and sounds
And untold feelings
Possessable
Here on earth
And in heaven.

There are sensitivities
To the feelings of others
So acute that the tiniest
Thought scarcely voiced
But crucial to the other
Resounds like
A thunder in our souls.

We possess a power
Of benevolence,
The ability to bestow
Unfathomable mercies
And enduring humanity.

Adventure is available
In each single cubby
And corner of existence.
Outrageous silliness
Is entirely possible.

Almost uncontainable
Rapture can be experienced
In the simplicity of daily living
With a wide open soul.

An infinite capacity
For astonishment
And perception
Of loveliness
Created by hand
And heart
Is native to us.

Sacred utterances
Can be heard
If one can listen
In the everyday world.

There are capacities
For honor and justice,
Integrity and ethics
And dignity beyond
What we've commonly
Known.

These abilities are seeable,
Are attainable, are knowable,
Are graspable by each
Living person regardless
Of anything at all.

Each of us have the divine
Right and honor to enter
These places and to know
These wonders.

Entrance to these worlds
Is the inborn privilege
Of each living soul
Here on earth.

We inherently possess
The innate magic
To open the gates
Of perception
To these worlds.

All of these treasures
Are the common
Endowment of each
Individual person
With no exception.

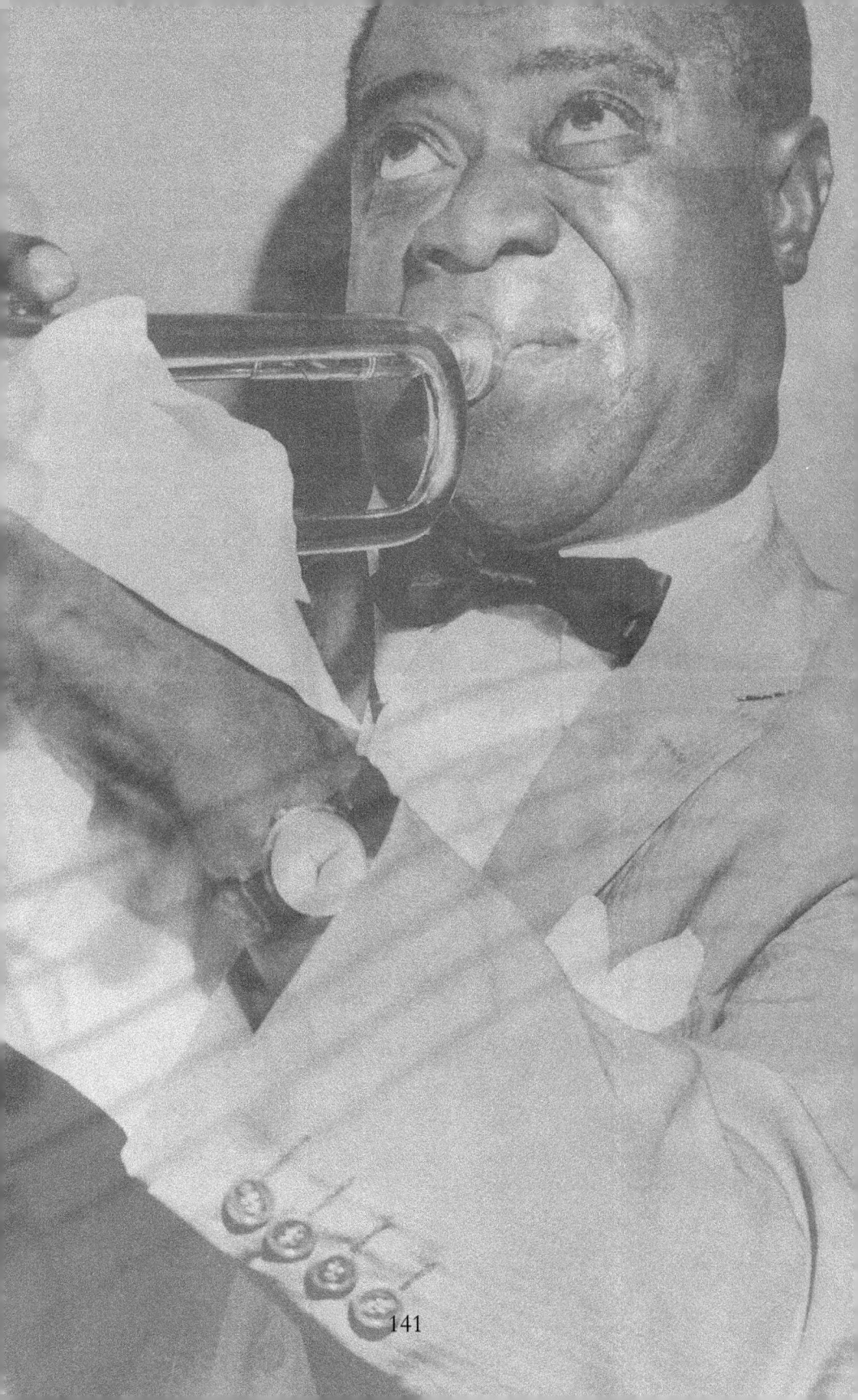

Chapter Seven

Old Age

Poppy

In the summer in this place
Ten thousand wild yellow Poppies
Grow on these steep hillsides.
Does it make a difference
If there is one Poppy less?

Yes, it does! Yes, it does!
Every single Poppy is needed.
Each child playing below is necessary.
Necessary lovers stand arm in arm
Beneath the necessary Oak Tree.

We need every lover, every child,
Every Daffodil, every Maple Tree
Turning colors in the crisp
New England October
Before the early snowfall.

Above all it is the unique
Aesthetic we bring to this earth
That will always remain
Though it changes shape
Ten thousand times.

We are always and ever aware
Of the metamorphosis.
Be we Oak or Elephant
Or old man walking alone,
We are alive and forever.

Ain't Goin' Nowhere

I can perceive you before me.
You seem to be an old woman
Sitting beneath the Maple Tree,
Serenely closing a lifespan.
Half here, half in eternity.
At least that's how it seems to me.

A body that you barely wear
Was vainly hoping you could stay.
But know you'll always be somewhere.
I'm certain you'll be OK.
You will be alive and aware.
In truth, you ain't going nowhere.

Necessary

Somehow each single living thing
Matters so much more intensely
Than it has ever mattered.
Somehow, this autumn evening
Has great need of me.

It is not that the sun would
Not set without my presence,
But somehow, I am
A necessary element,
Indelible and forever.

Laurel Tree

On Saturday when the Old Man passed,
The fishing boats were heading out to sea.
A cool, clear and sunny day was forecast.
Outside the window stood the Laurel Tree.
A quiet morning, my Old Man and me.

He said to me with peaceful certainty,
"I'm completed here you don't need to wait."
It was my Dad's usual courtesy.
He was there before me, yet separate.
"Son, I've a whole new lifetime to create."

Dignity

I went to see, Sparks, my old shipmate.
I came into his room reverently.
With great effort he pulled himself up straight.
His eyes recalled to me the open sea.
He took my hand in his with dignity.

Admiration

The beauty you are able to imbue,
An example of how a man can live.
For the time you've spent on earth we thank you.
Always listening, always responsive.
Your presence alone is restorative.

The Will to Create

Her vocal chords had grown brittle with age.
Still dreamed of singing on the concert stage.
My dear father when he could barely see
Painted down in the basement ardently.
Here on earth bodies grow old by and by,
But, a man's will to create does not die.

Bringing the Old Man Back

The old artist had lost his confidence.
He'd suffered terrible indignity.
The art critic said his art made no sense.
It shattered his aesthetic certainty.
He'd become criticism's casualty.

Found him slumped in a corner of a bar.
I told him his art made huge sense to me,
That his work was gifted and singular.
As he replied his eyes were watery.
He told me his purpose with intensity,
Which was to paint with utter clarity.
I could see the return of sanity.

How Grandma Saw It

Grandma's house seemed to be filled with kindness.
She was teaching her immigrant student
His English lessons with joy and lightness.
She laughed as she corrected his accent,
Then, he said it right to his amazement.

I knew that grandma had something to say.
She had that certain bright light in her eyes.
She was to turn eighty on Saturday.
"There're some things I'm beginning to realize
About what occurs when a person dies."

Light from the clerestory window above
Caused her face to seem to be translucent.
"It is about being able to love.
Help I've given is my accomplishment.
In this work, I value each moment spent.

"Keep helping until I can help no more."
I was touched deeply by her graciousness.
"I wasn't able to see this before.
You don't ever lose your helpfulness.
It's a purpose I will always possess."

Grandma Listens

Grandma has the treasured ability
To listen with unrestrained pure kindness,
Such an expression of affinity.
Her duplication is limitless.
I can so delight in her company.
I appreciate her huge heartedness.
I admire her immeasurably.

Empathy

She could see with her eyes but dimly.
Her hearing had gone many years ago.
But with her heart she could clearly see.
In some way, what we felt she would know.
My Grandma was made of empathy.

Not Too Late

She died a long, long time before she died.
Their criticism crushed her will to create
And suffocated her personal pride,
Made her feel utterly inadequate.
Just before she crossed to the other side,
Was a thing I had to communicate,
"All the beauty of your life will abide."
Immediately saw her reanimate.
I joyously knew it was not too late.

Salami and Eggs

Sitting alone in his special chair
In bitter protest to living's frailty,
Daddy felt it was utterly unfair
That he was unable to clearly see
The sun rising above the factory.

I brought him kosher salami and eggs,
The gift of a transistor radio,
A woolen blanket to warm his legs.
The hills of Pittsburgh were covered with snow.
He put his hand on my arm lovingly,
"Thank you for coming here to visit me."

Some Things I Need to Tell You

I think you are a much finer man
Than you even begin to comprehend.
I won't have you pass away until you
Have some inkling of your magnitude.

I was privileged to watch you work,
Able to watch you purvey your magic.
I could see the goodness in the incline
Of your frame as you bent down
To see what your son had to show you.

I am honored to have witnessed
Your unflagging kindness.
It was the extra listening
To the child I admired so.

I watched you at night working,
Grappling with a word, an idea.
Oblivious to anything around you.
How completely I'm able to love you.

In a quiet time I saw you looking,
Standing there with a purpose to see.
I am awed by how open handed
You are with your love.

Until you begin to grasp the value
Your being here with us has given,
You are not going anywhere at all.
I hope you understand that, my friend.

Chapter Eight

Immortality

Love is Stronger

We were able to create a bond
That would endure after our last breath
Into worlds and lifetimes beyond
For love is so much stronger than death.

The Last Mile

It is the last mile you walk alone.
You're all the person you have ever been.
Free from the tyranny of flesh and bone.
Completely aware, utterly serene.
An immortality you've long foreseen.

Relief

Knowing for sure that he was forever.
Red, amber and gold in the autumn leaf,
Garden flowers pale pink and lavender.
A glimpse of eternity although brief
Somehow engendered enormous relief.

Desert Sunflowers

Awestruck above a field of Desert Sunflowers,
The early morning sun rising warm behind me.
A floral prayer from God's own Book of Hours
That engenders a spiritual certainty
Of humankind's natural immortality.

By the Way

I am simultaneously aware
Of the blessings of living one more day
While preparing myself for an elsewhere.
I was never really human per se.
Being neither my flesh nor bones or hair.
I just may be immortal, by the way.

Be

To no longer be all that I am
Used to being and still to be.
To be without the cherished
Symbols of human existence.

To see, to hear, to touch and feel
Without the requirement of breath
Or the convenience of the senses.
Here and elsewhere simultaneously.

To possess that accustomed certainty
Of terrestrial love and belongingness
Without the familiar nape of her neck
As a known point of reference.

Seeing these once so comforting things
And yet no longer having need of them.
To step out beyond such things as:
Snow shovel, working gloves, icicle.

To carry both worlds inside of me
At the same time, alive in both,
The so fondly remembered world
And the ultimate, enduring, actual one.

The Ship Leaves the Harbor

I went home to the sea
Looking for peace of mind.
Recalling destiny.
Wisdom I need to find.

I had a tiny inkling
How it feels to be free.
I saw the truth lying
Tangled in the mystery.

The ship was in the harbor.
Sun rose early morning,
Knew what they'd come for
On this first day of Spring.

There's gold among the trinkets.
There is magic in the squalor.
These things a man forgets.
I have seen all this before.

Fog blew in from the sea.
Birds walked in the shallows.
A small glimpse of eternity.
Story the sea bird knows.

Music stirred my memory.
Basic human goodness.
Someone was kind to me.
I recalled a tenderness.

Walking to the threshold
Of possibility.
The future now unfolds,
A glimpse of eternity.

I could see a semblance
Of immortality.
I somehow found by chance
Backdoor of infinity.

The ship leaves the harbor.
Simultaneously,
I see what I'm here for.
Amazed at being free.

Transformation

Here's the worn pathway into the forest.
These living things tenderly remind me
Of the fruitful life with which I've been blessed.
Blossoms opening on the Cherry Tree,
New green on the hillsides as far as I can see.

I'm scarcely here on this beloved sphere.
Stone walkway, bench, garden gate, rake and hoe,
Earthly things that represent my stay here.
Preparing to discard the things I know,
One foot here, the other where I will go.

I'm willing to be the expected me
While taken up with transformation.
I'm here while simultaneously
Approaching another destination,
A new universe of my creation.

A Soundless Purr

To: Ingrid and Jazz

I thought I had lost you forever.
Two full weeks passed with you gone from me.
You were always the adventurer.
I received word spiritually.
Able to perceive a soundless purr,
I knew where you actually were.

A shelter kitten rushed right to me.
He tilted his small head just like you
And offered his paw courteously.
Felt unrestrained pure joy through and through.
He was light and cozy and carefree.
Was, in truth, you, but he was brand-new.

Beyond Human

To say goodbye
As darkness wells up
In the valley below.
To appear to be no more
All that I used to be
Or so it seems.

It is not death we fear.
It is obliteration.
The horror is to end,
To be no more.

What a shock to rise
Above the houses below
Unencumbered by the flesh.
To still be able to perceive
The children in the park below
Playing soccer on the pitch.

To be all that I've ever been.
Possessing all the love, care
Compassion, remembrance
That I have always had.

To live as a soul (again).
To feel without the aid
Of fingers or to see
Without the aid of eyes.

To perceive the vastness
Of the sky and the worlds
Beyond without limit.

To no longer be human per se.
Transforming into something
Or someone beyond human.

The sun is setting behind
The houses in quiet repose
On the rolling hills below.

Soon the rains will come.
Then in winter there'll be
The months of snow.

A thousand flowers
Surround my ashes.

I temporarily take
My leave.

In the ultimate
I am forever.

Death

Death is not
Just death
Just as life
Is not just
Life.
You die
Exactly
As you
Have
Lived.

The Unexpected World

Where have I come?
The hidden trail
Into the woodland,
Rosebush overgrown
Beside the path.
The green bench.
Rusted iron gate.
This place somehow
Utterly cherished.
These familiar
Earth things
That ever more tenderly
Remind me
Of who I am.

As I leave here
This stone wall,
These climbing vines,
These Lilac trees
Seem so tender
And necessary.
Appreciated
Beyond measure.
To apparently
No longer occupy
This temporary world
Takes my human
Breath away
For a moment.

To be no longer
Oriented by
The expected world
Or the usual me.
It is not my tufts
Of sparse white hair,
Crooked old fingers
Or my slowing gait.
I am ever more
Urgently taken up
With the task
Of restoration,
From temporal
To the infinite
Devoid of fear.

Retaining my familiar
Certainty of love
Without the nape
Of her neck
As a point
Of reference.
She is moving
From the pantry
To the oven.
Wintery day.
Smell of bread
Freshly baked.
Snow drifts
Beyond the window
Engulfing the barn.

Aware of these
Once so comforting,
Accustomed things
And yet no longer
Having need of them.
To step out beyond
These dear things.
To somehow carry
Both worlds
Inside of me
At the same time,
The expected world
And the actual,
Ultimate, enduring
Realm beyond.

Angel

I believe an angel did speak to me.
The angel was an old man in disguise.
He listened to my question patiently.
"Tell me, Sir, what happens when a man dies?"
Kindness was visible in his summer eyes.

He was sitting beneath a Lilac Tree.
"There's something of value to realize
Concerning the word—immortality.
You remain the same when the body dies.
It is not you! I need to emphasize."

Hearing this I felt a peace come over me.
I experienced enormous relief,
A grounded calmness and tranquility.
Glimpse of eternity, however brief.
Knowing this had value beyond belief.

Perhaps

Perhaps I will come across you
A long time hence,
Far beyond the stamina
Of the flesh.
I would know you then.

I will hear once again
Your same silly laugh
And the same dancing
Glow in your eyes
Will light up
That world as well.

Should I encounter you
Deep in forever,
I would unmistakably
Recognize you.

All of the wonder
That has always been you
Will continue to be you.
I will know you in forever
As I know you tonight.

As the sun sets
Behind the temple
Beside the river,
As friends throw
Flowers into the water,

I wish to assure you
That will be me,
That faint, urgent rustling
You hear or feel
At the outer edges
Of your awareness.

I promise you
That will be me
Just a wee bit
Beyond where
It's easy to see,
Greeting you.

Epilogue

It is such a gift to be able to convey the immortal human experience while still very much here in this expected world; to be present and beyond in the same instant. To no longer have need of these once so valued trappings. I have become more intensely aware of what endures beyond the cessation of the flesh in full awareness and perception, courage and love, long term friendships, courtesy and dignity, good deeds and listening.

What is important in this realm are the kindnesses that have been rendered, the compassion and empathy that has been exercised, the beauty and brilliance brought into this world. It is the power of empathy, above all, that survives lifetime to lifetime.

Remember what is actually valuable: the tenderness that exists naturally between human beings, our care of each other, the acknowledgement each to each that we have worth, that we matter, that we possess beauty and that we are welcome in our coming here and appreciated as we take our leave.

Glossary

Note: Webster's New World College Dictionary is the source for definitions unless otherwise noted.

Abide: to stand fast; remain; go on being. Page 79.

Aesthetic: of beauty. Pages 17, 22, 32, 37, 40, 66, 80.

Aesthetics: having a sense of the beautiful. Page 17. (Random House Webster's Unabridged Dictionary)

Annihilation: to destroy completely; put out of existence. Page 116.

Aspen Stand: a stand in this sense is: a growth of similar plants (usually trees) in a particular area; Quaking Aspen: a North American Poplar with small, flat-stemmed leaves that tremble in the slightest breeze. Page 24.

Note: There is a stand of Aspen Trees in Utah which is the largest known living thing on Earth. Nearly 50,000 stems protrude (stick out) from a single root system. The entire organism made up of the root structure and the trees that stem from it, covers over 100 acres and weighs 6000 tons. It is thought to have lived for 10s of thousands of years.

Asunder: in pieces; separate parts. Page 32. (Macmillan Dictionary For Students)

Audacity: boldness. Page 20. (Macmillan Dictionary for Students)

Bereft: suffering the death of a loved one. Page 5. (Merriam Webster On-line Dictionary)

Brevity: shortness of duration. Page 40. (Merriam Webster On-line Dictionary)

Caisson: A two wheeled wagon originally used to carry ammunition: also used to carry the casket in formal or state funerals. Page 29. (Your Dictionary)

Clerestory: highest story or uppermost portion of a wall; having a series of windows. Page 151. (Macmillan Dictionary for Students)

Commonality: a sharing as of common features or characteristics. Page 87.

Communion: an intimate relationship with deep understanding. Page 18.

Conjoined: joined together. (Cambridge Dictionary)

Construct: Something built or put together systematically. Page 96. (Collin's Dictionary)

Conveyance: that which transports or carries. Page 18. (The Macmillan Student Dictionary)

Crystalline: like crystal; clear and transparent. Page 105.

Dazzle: to arouse admiration by a brilliant display. Page 38.

Dazzlement: something that dazzles.

Devoid: completely without; empty or destitute. Page 79.

Disquietude: want of peace or tranquility; uneasiness; disturbance; agitation; anxiety. Page 66. (American Dictionary of the English Language, Noah Webster, 1828)

Eloquence: the quality of ... moving, or graceful expression. Page 46. (The American Heritage Dictionary)

Empathy: the ability to identify with or understand another's situation or feelings; empathy is a distinctly human capability. Pages 66, 181. (The American Heritage Dictionary)

Enmity: the bitter attitude or feelings of an enemy or of mutual enemies; hostility. Page 125.

Enraptured: to fill with great pleasure or delight. Page 41. (Macmillan Dictionary for Students)

Fairy: a being usually in human form and having magic powers, specif. one that is tiny, graceful, and delicate. Page 20.

Fairy Lanterns: also called Golden Fairy Lantern or Yellow Globe Lily. A flower having open branches, clusters of clear, yellow, egg shaped flowers. Native to Northern California. There are also rose colored and white species of this flower. *Little Worlds*, Page xxv and Page 14. (The Free Dictionary)

Fervency: having or showing great emotion or zeal. Page 109. (American Heritage Dictionary)

Glade: open space in a wood or forest. Page 58. (Macmillan Dictionary for Students)

Immortality: the quality of never ceasing to live or exist; exemption from death and annihilation; life destined to endure without end; as in the immortality of the human soul. Pages 2, 157, 160, 172, 177. (American Dictionary of the English Language, Noah Webster 1828)

Impunity: freedom from punishment, penalty, injury or loss. Page 105. (Macmillan Dictionary for Students)

Ineffable: that cannot be fully captured or described in words. Page 82. (Macmillan Dictionary for Students)

Jaded: worn out, tired; dulled as from over-indulgence. Page 25. (Macmillan Dictionary for Students)

Metamorphosis: complete or marked change, as of appearance, character, or condition. Page 144. (Macmillan Dictionary for Students)

Milestone: a significant or important event in history, in a person's career, etc. Page 61.

Mon amie: my friend (French). Page 29.

Presage: to foretell or predict. Page 51. (American Heritage Dictionary)

Pristine: still pure; uncorrupted; unspoiled. Page 105.

Replete: completely filled; full. Page 77. (American Dictionary of the English Language, Noah Webster, 1828)

Schmo: one who is foolish, dull or naïve. (Yiddish). Page 44. (Macmillan Dictionary for Students)

Stately: dignified, majestic. Page 18.

Stymied: to bring to or keep at a standstill; frustrate; block. Page 5. (Macmillan Dictionary for Students)

Transience: of temporary or brief duration. Page 145. (Macmillan Dictionary for Students)

Translucent: partially transparent, as frosted glass. Page 151.

Ubiquitous: present, or seeming to be present, everywhere at the same time. Page 25.

Unflagging: not wavering or failing; untiring; sustained Page 156. (Macmillan Dictionary for Students)

Vermilion: bright red color. Page 19. (Macmillan Dictionary for Students)

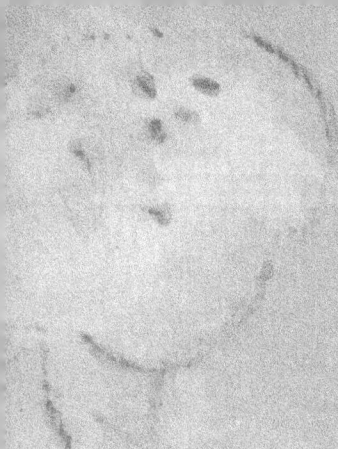

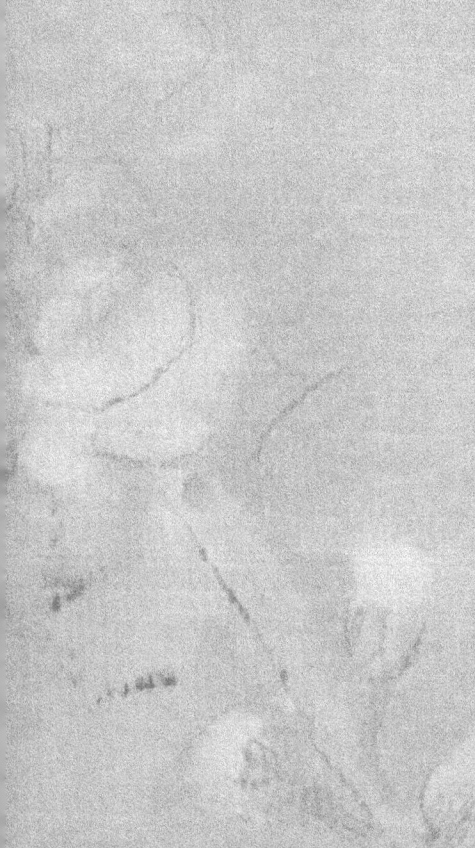

Acknowledgements

My extreme gratitude to my wife, Connie, for her constant support over years. She has brought out the best there is in me as a writer and as a man. The artist, Diane Woods, has illustrated this book providing a visual dimension that moves the written communications to another level. My appreciation for her duplication of the work has no limits. I wish to thank educator, Ingrid Gudenas, for her unflagging support and encouragement and belief in the work. The help of Stephanie Cavalli with social media has been invaluable in making the writing available to a much larger audience. My thanks to my publishers, Patricia Ross and George Gluchowski for their early on belief in the work and their assistance in bringing it into the world. Thank you, Ronda Taylor for your caring and perceptive design of all of my books. Above all I want to acknowledge author and educator L. Ron Hubbard from whom I received my first inkling of the enormity of the human spirit.

Special Thanks

There is a very special community online called Pixabay. Their stated purpose is to empower creators...how awesome is that! I have woven treasures from their site into *Little Worlds* and the reviews we have gotten demonstrate the power of our mutual creation. Here are just some of these contributors.

Page 18 Weightless Elephant by PIRO4D
Page 20 Antique Fairy Tale Book Cover by Oberholster Venita
Page 26 Free-Photos (smiling woman)
Page 45 PublicDomainPictures
Pages 64 and 65 Gerd Altmann
Pages 85 and 86 Gerd Altmann
Page 115 David Mark
Page 121 nahidsheikh31
Page 134 Mariamichelle
Page 155 StockSnap
Page 160 Stefan Keller

Thank you all.
Diane Woods

Note: The portrait of Sarah Bernhardt on page 29 is by Alphonse Mucha. The painting on page 95 is by John and Abigail Adams' great-great-grandson, John Quincy Adams.

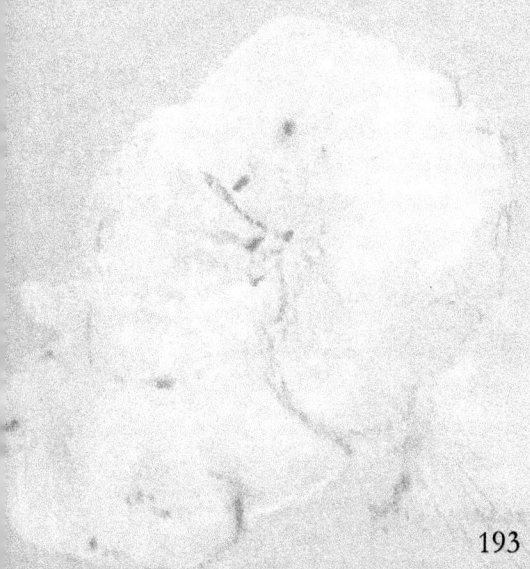